THE BUTTERFLY BOOK

Written by CYNTHIA OVERBECK
Illustrated by SHARON LERNER

LERNER PUBLICATIONS COMPANY
MINNEAPOLIS, MINNESOTA

LIBRARY OF CONGRESS CATALOGING IN PUBLICATION DATA

Overbeck, Cynthia.
The butterfly book.

(An Early Nature Picture Book)
SUMMARY: Text and illustrations introduce the character-
istics of ten familiar butterflies and the four stages in the life
cycle of the butterfly.

1. Butterflies — Pictorial works — Juvenile literature.
[1. Butterflies] I. Lerner, Sharon. II. Title.

QL544.2.093 1978   595.7'89   78-7235
ISBN 0-8225-1111-8

AN EARLY NATURE PICTURE BOOK

Copyright © 1978 by Lerner Publications Company

All rights reserved. International copyright secured. Manufactured
in the United States of America. Published simultaneously in Canada
by J. M. Dent & Sons (Canada) Ltd., Don Mills, Ontario.

International Standard Book Number: 0-8225-1111-8
Library of Congress Catalog Card Number: 78-7235

2 3 4 5 6 7 8 9 10 85 84 83 82 81 80

CONTENTS

Almost anywhere you go on a spring or summer day, you are sure to see butterflies. These bright winged insects fly wherever there are flowers and sunshine. Hundreds of different kinds of butterflies live in North America. In this book you will see just a few of them.

Butterflies are beautiful as adults. But when they begin their lives, they are not so pretty. A butterfly must go through four stages of life in order to become a winged adult. In each stage, its body looks completely different. The story of how a butterfly grows and changes is one of nature's most amazing tales.

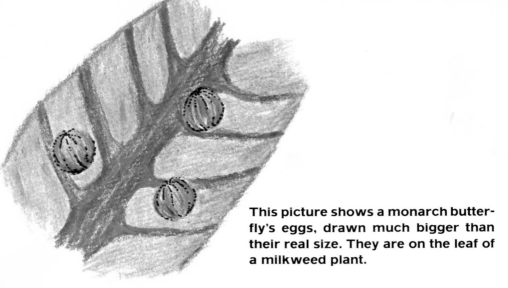

This picture shows a monarch butter-fly's eggs, drawn much bigger than their real size. They are on the leaf of a milkweed plant.

These pictures show the growth of only one kind of butterfly—the monarch. But all butterflies grow in the same way. Every butterfly begins its life as a tiny egg, no bigger than the head of a pin. The female butterfly lays her eggs on the leaf of a plant. Each kind of butterfly chooses a special plant. Its leaves will serve as food for the young after they have hatched.

In a few days, the eggs break open. Out of each egg comes a tiny, wormlike caterpillar. It is only about 1/8 inch (3 mm) long. This crawling thing will someday be a lovely butterfly! But first it has a job to do. That job is to eat. The caterpillar never goes away from the plant on which it was hatched. It stays right there and gobbles the leaves until it doubles in size.

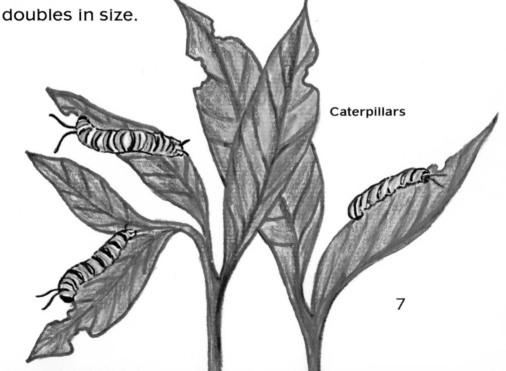

Caterpillars

7

After about two weeks, the caterpillar suddenly stops eating. It hangs upside down from a leaf or twig and keeps very still. Then it begins to twist and squirm. Off comes its skin. The body of the caterpillar, now called a **pupa** (PYOO-puh), is soft and unprotected. But a hard shell, or **chrysalis** (KRIS-ah-liss), soon forms around the pupa. For about 10 days, the chrysalis hangs from the leaf, showing no signs of life. But inside, an amazing change is taking place. The pupa is becoming a butterfly. Its body is changing and its wings are forming. Finally the chrysalis splits open. Slowly, a butterfly works its way out! Soon it spreads its bright new wings and sails over gardens and fields.

This chrysalis has turned dark. Now you can see through it. You can see the wings of the monarch butterfly inside.

This monarch chrysalis has just been formed. It is green with gold spots.

MONARCH

This beautiful monarch came out of its chrysalis in the spring. Monarchs are one kind of butterfly that almost everybody has seen. In summer they fly slowly around gardens all over the United States and Canada. When winter comes, some kinds of butterflies hibernate (HY-ber-nate). This means that they fold their wings and go into a deep sleep that lasts until springtime. Other butterflies spend the winter as a chrysalis. But monarchs do something different. Like birds, they migrate (MY-grate), or fly south for the winter. In the fall, thousands of monarchs gather in large groups and fly to warmer places in the south. When spring returns, the monarchs fly back toward the north.

SOUTHERN DOGFACE

The southern dogface gets its unusual name because of the way it looks. The yellow shapes on its front wings look a little like the side view of a dog's head, complete with eyes! This "dogfaced" butterfly lives east of the Rocky Mountains and as far south as Central America.

Like all butterflies, the southern dogface has a slender body. Its body is divided into three parts—the abdomen, thorax, and head. The abdomen is the long, thin "tail" part. The thorax is the wider middle part. The butterfly's four wings are attached to its thorax. On the butterfly's head are two feelers, called **antennae** (an-TEN-ee). The antennae end in tiny knobs, or clubs.

GREAT PURPLE HAIRSTREAK

The great purple hairstreak is one of the most beautiful of all the butterflies. As it darts over open fields, the sunlight shines on its richly colored wings. It can be found in most of the eastern United States and sometimes as far west as California.

The caterpillar of the great purple hairstreak feeds on mistletoe leaves. The adult butterfly, like most other butterflies, eats the sweet nectar, or juice, of flowers. All butterflies have long, thin tongues that are hollow inside. When a butterfly lands on a flower, it pushes its tongue into the center. Butterflies use their tongues like straws to drink the nectar of flowers.

PAINTED LADY

Painted lady butterflies live in almost every part of the United States and Canada. Their bright patterned wings are strong as well as pretty. Painted ladies need strong wings in order to migrate. You have read that monarch butterflies migrate every winter to a warm place. But painted ladies do not migrate to get away from the cold. Instead, they migrate to find something to eat. Sometimes the number of painted ladies in one place becomes so great that there are no longer enough thistle or hollyhock plants to feed the new caterpillars. When this happens, huge swarms of painted ladies fly hundreds of miles to a place where there is more food.

16

GREAT SPANGLED FRITILLARY

The great spangled fritillary (FRIT-eh-lair-ee) is one of a group called the **brush-footed** butterflies. They are called that because their short front legs are covered with tiny brush-like hairs. Like all butterflies, the great spangled fritillary has three pairs of legs.

The upper surface of the great spangled fritillary's wings, shown in the picture, has a pattern of brown and black marks. The underside has many silver spots. In the Ozark Mountains, there is a legend about this butterfly. People say that if you see one, you will have good luck. They say that for every silver spot you see on its wings, you will receive a silver coin.

SPRING AZURE

In early spring, the first butterfly that you are likely to see is the dainty little spring azure. It is named for its lovely sky-blue, or azure (AZH-uhr), color. Its name also tells us in what season it appears. Sometimes called the **common blue**, it can be found almost anywhere in North America.

The caterpillar of the spring azure eats the buds of flowering dogwood, blueberry, and other bushy plants. This caterpillar has an interesting friendship with ants. On its body are two tiny tubes filled with a sweet green liquid called **honeydew**. Ants often follow the caterpillar and drink its honeydew. In return, the ants help to protect the caterpillar from spiders, wasps, and other enemies.

VICEROY

When you first see a viceroy butterfly, you may mistake it for a monarch. These two butterflies are almost identical twins. Only when you compare them closely will you see that the viceroy has an extra black stripe across each back wing and bigger black markings. The viceroy is lucky to look so much like the monarch. Birds that like to eat butterflies know that the monarch does not make a good meal. Its body has a bitter taste. When birds see the bright colors and patterns of the monarch's wings, they stay away. The viceroy's body does not have a bitter taste. But when birds see its wings, they think it is a bitter-tasting monarch, and they leave it alone.

PEARLY EYE

The brown pearly eye butterfly can be found in woodlands all over the eastern part of North America, from Canada to Florida. But it is not easy to spot. It likes to fly in the shade of the forest trees, or in the evening when the light is fading. Its brown color blends in well with the shadows.

In their forest homes, pearly eyes sometimes become fighters. A male pearly eye will often pick out a particular tree as his own "territory." He will return to the same tree every day. When other butterflies try to come near, he will chase them away or even fight them.

EASTERN TIGER SWALLOWTAIL

With its wingspan of up to 6.5 inches (16 cm), the eastern tiger swallowtail is one of the largest of the North American butterflies. Its black and yellow wing markings remind us of a tiger's stripes. The "tails" on its back wings look like the tail of the lovely bird called the swallow. Eastern tiger swallowtails may have many different kinds of markings. Usually the females look very different from the males. The females' wings have darker colors and fewer markings. Such dull coloring helps to hide the female butterfly from birds or insects that might attack. The female must be safe in order to do the important job of laying her eggs.

MOURNING CLOAK

The yellow and brown mourning cloak is another butterfly that we see early in the spring. The adult butterflies, which are found everywhere in the United States, hibernate all winter long. They come out in the spring to eat tree sap and flower nectar. Mourning cloaks lay their eggs on the twigs of willow, poplar, and elm trees.

Mourning cloak butterflies have an interesting way of protecting themselves from birds and insects. They fool their enemies by "playing dead." When mourning cloaks are frightened, they become so still and limp that their enemies think that they are already dead. Then the birds or insects leave the butterflies alone.

BUTTERFLIES ALL AROUND YOU

This spring or summer, see what kinds of butterflies you can find in your neighborhood. You can also look for the caterpillars that will turn into butterflies. Try to learn what plants each kind of caterpillar eats. This will help you to know where to look for the little creatures.

It is fascinating to watch these insects in their natural surroundings. If you take time and look carefully, you can find a whole new world in your garden or neighborhood park. You can discover the bright and beautiful world of butterflies.

HOW BIG ARE BUTTERFLIES?

Spring Azure

Painted Lady

Monarch

Eastern
Tiger
Swallowtail

(Butterflies shown here are one-half actual size.)

Butterfly	Average Wingspan
SPRING AZURE	1" (2.5 cm)
GREAT PURPLE HAIRSTREAK	1.4"(3.5 cm)
PEARLY EYE	1.8"(4.5 cm)
PAINTED LADY	2.1"(5.3 cm)
SOUTHERN DOGFACE	2.3"(5.8 cm)
VICEROY	2.7"(6.8 cm)
MOURNING CLOAK	3" (7.5 cm)
GREAT SPANGLED FRITILLARY	3.5"(8.8 cm)
MONARCH	3.7"(9.3 cm)
EASTERN TIGER SWALLOWTAIL	5.2"(13 cm)